THE WEATHER

Ed Catherall

Science is Fun

Balls and Balloons	**Growing Plants**
Bulbs and Batteries	**Light and Dark**
Clay Play	**Mirrors and Lenses**
Colours	**Our Pets**
Floating and Sinking	**Sand Play**
Fun with Magnets	**The Weather**
Fun with Wheels	**Wind Play**

5888

Illustrations by David Anstey

First published in 1986 by
Wayland (Publishers) Ltd
61 Western Road, Hove
East Sussex BN3 1JD, England

© Copyright 1986 Wayland (Publishers) Ltd

British Library Cataloguing in Publication Data
Catherall Ed,
The weather. – (Science is fun)
1. Weather – Juvenile literature
I. Title   II. Series
551.5   QC981.3
ISBN 0–85078–860–9

Phototypeset by
Kalligraphics Ltd, Redhill, Surrey
Printed in Italy by
G. Canale & C.S.p.A., Turin
Bound in the U.K. by
The Bath Press, Avon

CONTENTS

Today's weather   4
Your clothes   5
Sports and the weather   6
Weather forecasts   7
Keeping a weather diary   8
Clouds   9
Cloud types   10
Cloud shapes   11
The speed of clouds   12
The wind and the weather   13
Our changing winds   14
Wind speed   15
The Beaufort scale   16
Today's temperature   17
Ground temperatures   18
Water temperatures   19
Raindrops   20
Making a rain gauge   21
Thunder storms   22
Storms   23
Glossary and Index   24

Today's weather

What is the weather like today?
Do you like today's weather?
How do you think the weather will change today?

What was the weather like yesterday?
What do you think the weather will be like tomorrow?

Where do you go for your holidays?
What kind of weather do you expect there?

Your clothes

Are your clothes right for today's weather?
What do you wear to school when it is hot?
What do you wear when it is raining?
What do you wear when it is cold?

What will you do if the weather changes today?

What clothes are worn in the Antarctic?
What clothes are worn in the desert?

Sports and the weather

List the sports that are played in winter.
List the sports that are played in summer.
Which sports are played in all kinds of weather?
Which sports are stopped by the weather?

What special clothing is worn for
each of the sports you listed?

What weather is best for sailing, windsurfing and
hang-gliding?

6

Weather forecasts

When did you last see or hear a weather forecast?

Which weather forecasters do you like best?
What do you like about this forecaster?

Do you think weather forecasts are accurate?
Did today's forecast affect your choice of clothes?

Keeping a weather diary

Find a scrap book that you can use for a
weather diary.

Record the weather each day in your diary.
Look for pictures to put in your diary.
Include newspaper cuttings in your diary.

Leave plenty of space so that you can make many
recordings each day.

Clouds

Are there clouds in the sky today?
Never look directly at the sun.
It will damage your eyes.
How much of the sky is covered with clouds today?
Are all the clouds at the same height?
Are any of the clouds man-made?
Look for factory smoke.
Are there airplane trails in the sky?
Where are these planes going?

Cloud types

Collect pictures of clouds to put in your weather diary.

Which clouds give rain showers?
Which clouds give constant rain?
Which clouds never give rain?

Which cloud types are there in the sky today?
Record these cloud types in your weather diary.

Cloud shapes

What shape are the clouds today?

What strange shapes can you see in the clouds?
Use your imagination: can you see faces and
animal shapes in the clouds?

Watch the clouds change shape.
Look at the edges of the clouds.
What is happening?

The speed of clouds

Wait for a sunny day with small clouds in the sky.
Stand where you can see a long distance.

Watch the shadow of a cloud.
How big is the shadow?
A cloud's shadow is the same size as the cloud.

In which direction is the shadow moving?
Watch the edge of the shadow.
Notice how fast the shadow moves.

The wind and the weather

In which direction is the wind blowing today?
What is the weather like today?
Record the wind direction each day in your
weather diary.
Show the wind direction as a compass point.

Which way does the wind blow on cold days?
Which way does the wind blow on wet days?

WIND DIRECTION FOR
SEPTEMBER

Our changing winds

Which way are the clouds moving today?
Are all the clouds moving in the same direction?
Are all the clouds moving at the same speed?

Which way is the wind moving near the ground?
Watch smoke or a weather vane.

Hold up one wet finger.
Which way is the wind blowing?
How many ways can you think of to
find the wind's direction?

Wind speed

Watch a flag flying in the wind.
Which direction is the wind blowing?

Look at the flag.
How strong is the wind blowing?

Look at the effect of today's wind on the trees.
What is happening?
How strong do you think the wind is blowing?

The Beaufort scale

DESCRIPTION	WIND SPEED (MPH)	WIND SPEED (KPH)	SIGNS
LIGHT BREEZE	4–7	6.4–11.3	LEAVES MOVE, WIND JUST FELT
MODERATE BREEZE	13–18	20.8–29	SMALL BRANCHES MOVE, DUST RAISED
STRONG BREEZE	25–31	40.2–49.9	LARGE BRANCHES MOVE
FRESH GALE	39–46	62.8–74.1	TWIGS BREAK OFF BRANCHES
STRONG GALE	47–54	75.7–86.9	LARGE BRANCHES BREAK
STORM	64–75	103.4–120.7	WIDESPREAD DAMAGE

The chart above is known as the Beaufort Scale.
Estimate the speed of the wind today.
Record this wind speed in your weather diary.
Do not measure sudden wind gusts.
Record any changes of wind speed during the day.
Is the wind getting weaker or stronger?

Today's temperature

Listen to or watch the weather forecast.
What temperature is forecast for today?
Find a thermometer.
Measure the air temperature in the sun.
Measure the air temperature in the shade.

Record the air temperature in the shade each hour.
What do you notice?
Always measure the temperature at the same time
for your weather diary.

Ground temperatures

On a hot day measure the air temperature in the sun and in the shade.

Look for different kinds of ground.
Measure the temperature of grass in the sun and in the shade.
Measure the temperature of bare soil, concrete, tar and leaf litter.
What do you notice?

Water temperatures

Put an equal amount of water into
two plastic bowls.
Put one bowl in the sun.
Put the other bowl in the shade.

Measure the water temperature every hour.
Measure the ground temperature near the bowls.
What do you notice?
What happens if you use more water?

Raindrops

Hold a sheet of newspaper out in the rain.
Catch a few raindrops on the paper.
Notice the size of the spots the raindrops make on the paper.

Place a saucer out in the rain.
Watch the raindrops splash in the saucer.
Which way is the wind blowing the rain?

Watch raindrops run down a window.

20

Making a rain gauge

Find a plastic funnel that just fits into the top of
a straight-sided jar.
You have made a rain gauge.

Place your rain gauge outside to collect the rain.
Use a ruler to measure the depth of
rain water in your jar.
Record this level in your weather diary.

Empty the rain gauge after measuring the depth.

J551·5

Thunder storms

What clouds do you see during a thunder storm?
Lightning is a big electrical spark.
Thunder is the noise made by this spark.

How many seconds after you see the lightning
do you hear the thunder?
If it is 3 seconds the lightning is 1 km away.
If it is 5 seconds the lightning is 1 mile away.

Storms

Collect newspaper reports of bad weather to put in
your weather diary.
Record where this bad weather was.
Record how much damage was done during
the storm.
What was the wind speed during the storm?

Collect pictures of weather in other countries.

GLOSSARY

Compass An instrument that always shows where north is.

Diary A book where you can write down what happens each day.

Estimate To guess the size, amount, or price of something.

Funnel A tube with a wide opening for pouring liquids into bottles.

Rain gauge An instrument which measures rainfall.

Thermometer An instrument which measures temperature.

Weather forecast A programme on television or radio, which tells you what the weather will be like.

Weather vane An instrument which shows wind direction.

INDEX

Air temperature   17
Beaufort scale   16
Clothes   5, 6
Cloud shapes   11
Cloud speed   12
Cloud types   10
Clouds   9
Forecast   7, 17
Ground temperature   18
Lightning   22
Rain direction   20

Rain gauge   21
Raindrops   20
Sport   6
Sun   9
Thunder storms   22, 23
Water temperature   19
Weather diary   8, 16, 17, 21, 23
Wind   13
Wind direction   14, 15, 20
Wind speed   15